# YOU DON'T HAVE TO GO TO MARS FOR LOVE

Also by Yona Harvey

*Hemming the Water*

# YOU DON'T HAVE TO GO TO MARS FOR LOVE

## Yona Harvey

Four Way Books

Tribeca

Library of Congress Cataloging-in-Publication Data

Names: Harvey, Yona, author.
Title: You don't have to go to mars for love / Yona Harvey.
Other titles: You do not have to go to mars for love
Description: New York : Four Way Books, [2020] | Series: A Stahlecker
series selection | Summary: "The poems document the Afro-futuristic
journey of an unnamed, female protagonist passing through various
districts in space"-- Provided by publisher.
Identifiers: LCCN 2019054595 | ISBN 9781945588563 (trade paperback)
Subjects: LCGFT: Poetry.
Classification: LCC PS3608.A78928 Y68 2020 | DDC 811/.6--dc23
LC record available at https://lccn.loc.gov/2019054595

This book is manufactured in the United States of America and printed on
acid-free paper.

Four Way Books is a not-for-profit literary press. We are grateful for the assistance
we receive from individual donors, public arts agencies, and private foundations.

This publication is made possible with public funds from the
National Endowment for the Arts

and from the New York State Council on the Arts, a state agency,

We are a proud member of the Community of Literary Magazines and Presses.

Contents

for Ua and Aaron

"Tonight I feel the stars are out
to use me for target practice."
                              —Yusef Komunyakaa

# THAT

I grew up with pickles. I slept in
the attic (cigarettes, sheets laced with
smoke). The heat of my father's
brother's old room. Larry Blackmon
painted for effect & Chaka Khan's lips
more like a kiss if a kiss could walk
when it came to life. If a kiss
could have hips & legs & ass—
well, I wanted that.
& if the colors could sweat & strip
me down to my slip, well,
I wanted that, too. Nobody knew
what I was thinking up there.
Though, maybe, they wanted that. That.

# SEGREGATION CONTINUUM

*after Ella Baker & Glenn Ligon*

layered in black on black on white canvas
we who believe in freedom cannot rest
looking at the way we look looking forward
stepping back by way of upturned neck by way
of three steps back looking black coded by way
of black modes by way of reconstruction by way
of insurrection by way of colored fountains by way
of elected democrats or elected aristocrats
it is obvious we are a presence
though we have been discomforted
at school gates at rental offices at museum entrances
even we cannot rest who believe in freedom
we are to some an irritant an ire some tire some lot
we do not subscribe just because something comes
out of a leader's mouth out of the mouth of a tyrant
so we are too difficult we are much too difficult
we are much too aware we are much too marked
we are all that matter to us that matter
we are the most comforting presence by way of
nod by way of pound by way of sup
we are always fashionable when we do not try
we do not try to insult except when we do
but we do not hesitate to speak of the things
about which we agree or disagree we participate
at the level of our thinking by way of our thinking

by way of our mass expression
we who believe in freedom cannot rest
where once hundreds & even thousands of we
ordinary people had taken a position—that made us—
very uncomfortable when we decided for instance
to walk rather than take the bus

# THE BASELINE

I was in a neurosurgeon's waiting room awaiting Aaro's test results—
he'd slammed his skull on the basketball court & his pupils pulsed
cartoony, black spirals & asterisks, & loony exclamations. His dizzy
days had placed us in the clipboard's teeth, snapping. NBA season—
the finals—& Doctor Phil was interviewing a boy who'd killed his
mother—bashed his mother's head with a sledgehammer & set her
house on fire.

"It's ritual," said the doc, "It's self-soothing."

To bash someone's head? To set a house on fire?

Okay, Doc. Okay, America. Okay.

I forget how daytime gnaws us till evening if we linger too long in its
jaws. Everything wrong with us seemed to glow from the insides of
a flat screen. I wondered what was up next? A razor? A switchblade?
A machete? Little bits of bone? The boy's little blonde brother, nearly
dying, too?

Okay, Homemakers. Okay, Ratings.

A nurse walked Aaro to an exam room. Free throws & foul shots
chatter. Winners & losers. Favorite players. LeBron James slept

somewhere between games. How many times had Aaro hit his head in the past few years?

"Bring it in," Aaro said when I joined him. "Chill," he said.

Did this mean he was the kind of son who'd hug his mother tightly before turning away? The kind of kid who shrugged off blond boys, the kind of kid who'd leave home at twelve & assemble a band & adorn his fro with feathers & cowries & swear he learned the birds & the bees from Netflix, *Grand Theft Auto* & the Internet?

Okay, Worst Fears.

What was the last thing Aaro remembered? A thwack. The court's distant border. I forget how competitive he gets. I forget how fragile. Diagnosis: no games for three weeks. Supervised exercise. Rest. Okay, Inevitable. My mother didn't care much for television. "Turn that stuff off," she'd say. "Talk to me." I forget how mustache begins in shadow, how hairlines fade gradually. What makes a child turn? One year, Cleveland fans burned LeBron's jersey.

Okay, Christians. Okay, Cavaliers.

I forget how every son leaves us at least once. I forget how quiet a house without television. Son, don't bring any spiders home. Or lovers or trash talk. I forget how we bring those, anyway. I forget how hypnotic the television.

Eat your dinner, son. Eat your dinner.

# SONNET FOR A TALL FLOWER BLOOMING AT DINNERTIME

Southern Flower, I want to quote the bard,
to serenade you, to raise a glass to you.
Long & tall you are always parched
& hungry. You wobble in strong winds, you
puff your bright hair when it rains, you
toss off the lint of dandelions, you
lean into the evening haunts
with your indifferent afro. You
were born in the old-world city, the invisible
dark-girl city, the city that couldn't hold
a candle, a straight pin, a slave-owner's sins
to you. You are the most beautiful
       dark that hosts the most private sorrows
       & feeds the hungriest ghosts.

# "I worked hard so my girls didn't have to serve nobody else like I did except God"

*after Elizabeth Clark-Lewis*

Candy-colored bulbs frame a girl for a holiday.
If the wicked call from the other side, she doesn't hear. Blinds shut. Devices
blink & twitter. Before it's too late, her mother snaps a picture—anticipates
angst & oddly angled aches, strawberry letters. "Whatevers."
The mother will mark the photo tomorrow. Sign. Seal. "We're all well!"


—one of the last acceptable print messages. Meanwhile, "Soup
for dinner, again?" What else? It's winter. Herbal constellations swivel in froth. Stir.
She samples with a lean near bowing. Steam on closed eyelids.
Mothers ought to give thanks.
*Simeon,* she thinks instead, & then: her long-gone grandmother's
tattered Bible, the daughter's overdue library book
concerning States' rights. Why's that? She's hardly felt
hated. X's & O's glow in the daughter's palm *Look
how easy,* the daughter often says. She is patient with her mother. Blessed
be the child at the center of snow & flu season. She flew past
blessings long ago. So far from a little girl, really.

# NECESSARILY

*after Gwendolyn Brooks*


She's got a hundred & two temperature,

                    delivery room nurses said. You're

     gonna live, though—long enough

                        to know you're going

to go as quickly as you came, gonna

              make your mother swear by you, going to

     shake your Bible with red-tipped nails

                     before you vanish

into Chicago South Side skies that bleed—

             not like watercolor, not like a wound, not

     like a fat, bitten plum—not necessarily.

                  No, not necessarily.

Nothing that precious or predictable. Speak

             nicely to others & they will nicely

     speak to you, your mother said.

               No, not so, you said fairly

close to the end. No time to wait for mother's

           ride home or for saviors, coming soon.

# PERFORMANCE PERM / "I'D RATHER BE A BLIND GIRL"

*after Etta James, Live from San Francisco, 1994*

Lord, Etta—

*Something told me* My mama waited too long to mention *it was over. When I saw you with that girl & yall was talking* her neighbor *saw you with that girl & yall was talking* cueing your music all summer long *Something deep down* —scotch *Something deep down* & water, *Something deep down* gin & *Something deep down* you, *Something deep down said / it was over / When I saw you / gone & cry girl* she knew how to keep company. All my muscles *deep down* undone now. Girl, I shoulda *Something told me Something told me Something told me* had your name. Et-ta, Et-ta. Et-ta. *& I'd rather.* Let the men holler after me, *& I'd rather* let the women shake their heads. *Something told me* relish the cool *I was just sitting here thinking* of a single ice cube *thinking* melted *thinking* at the bar counter, *thinking thinking thinking thinking* far from conversation. You sang the songs *& I'm scared to be by myself.* Your mama warned you not to—*& I'd rather & I'd rather & I'd rather & I'd rather &*—*be by myself.* Yo. Yo. Hmmm. *& yo. I see yall know what I'm talking bout when I say,* sweet sin & excess, *& yo. I see yall know what I'm talking bout when I say,* Cigarettes *& yo. & yo. & yo. & yo* the smoke when I look down into my glass & say

12

Yo, Summer. *Yo* & *yo* & revealing its *Yo* damp sky, *Yo. Yo. Yo. Yo. Yo. &*

*yo.* When I saw you with that same person *& I'm scared to be by myself.* &

holler after me. Too long. Something told me.

# LIKE A MAGPIE

When she comes running over like that. Like an apology. Like she must. When she seems frightened. When she seems wounded. When she seems to have been bullied. In a park. Just like this one. She'd been showing off. Like a high yellow song. Like now. But still. She seems fragile & thin. In the gray cloak of winter. When she should go. Maybe start all over. Where she started. Where it all first sugared. & turned black. Cavernous. Cavity. An exaggeration. Just a little dip. A cut of air. Like a mistake. What we say to one another. Stays out there. What we do also. An apology—

is not an eraser. Maybe a filling. A cover. For words spoken in haste. Or maybe. With purpose. With fear & anger. If she should go now. How would her flock know to find her? With a new family? With purpose? With fear & anger? Where she started. Like a magpie out of orbit. Dismissed. All that energy. All those slicked-back feathers. They looked like no feathers at all. Naked. Out of purpose. Where should she go? Like a mistake. Where she started. She wants to start all over. But.

Who am I to say? The eye is often mistaken. Or is it the mind? Always eager to interpret. To turn one's mouth. Every witcha way. But what does the eye know? What it seeks. The magpie twirling in the park. Stumbling. Like a liar. The gelled-back feathers. Was she caught in the snow? Just seconds. Before. Working to know. What one can never. With purpose? A cover. For words spoken. In haste. & anger. She seemed hurt. She seemed. Like a magpie. Like a liar. But I might be wrong. What my eye saw. Where I started. Just seconds before. A lost thing.

She seemed fragile. Thinner than ever. Preoccupied. Hungry. Like someone had made a mistake. Had they? Always eager. She wanted to start all over. We all want that. From time to time. A cut of air. A cut of the eye. All that sadness. Just seconds. After. Let's erase. With purpose? With gladness? A map. Put your hammer away. If a woman seems fragile. Try to focus. On a magpie. On a blend-in bird.

A lost thing. Happens. The eye can miss. Just seconds. She seemed fragile. Different. Like a high yellow sadness. Like someone. A lost thing. From time to time. A tiny hole. A little dip. Shield her from air. Like a second. In snow. Without a flock.

# BOY IN THE FOREST BETWEEN LIVING & LEAVING

*after Virginia Hamilton*


—That time—
            when boys who were down said, "down," & dressed
in such a way that their out-of-school clothes resembled
their night- &-day clothes & play clothes & on-the-court
                              or on-the-field clothes
        those don't-wanna-be-like-them clothes

—that time—
            one boy walked alongside the dark in his dark
knee-length shorts & bulb-bright shirt that inflated
& deflated whenever the wind entered or exited the sleeves
as if to say when puffed, *This is the man he will become,* &
when shrunken, *But he is only on the verge now,*
                       & it appeared as if a narrow flame
were flaring & flickering & walking or floating alongside
a long stretch of road
      there were no street signs or landmarks
just the dark stretching
away from itself & the boy walking off walking away
rather than toward anyone or anything
though maybe that's the way it felt when one watched another
walking from a distance, the boy kept moving
& each time it seemed as though he might stop to check
if he were headed in the right direction or wipe his hands on his shirt

19

or listen for rickety trucks or long rope troubles that wickedly come
                              the boy never stopped
not even to pull
his shoestrings tighter
which wouldn't have mattered
because he wore no shoes or socks
& the patch of trees ahead outblacked the sky
& announced themselves & bent & swore *we are safe trees*
for they knew their branches had been defiled & low-hanging & long-
    broken & eased into
the earth the trees were weary from what they had seen
from how they had been used & could not account for the crimes
of men who had not yet atoned—
so they bent their leaf-thick heads & revealed a new path for the boy
that he might make his way to live alongside long-living boys
& just like that
the boy was in a forest
& the road disappeared behind him
& the boy walked further toward the shelter
of more trees away from the doomed
& damned & hunted & heckled & haunted & hounded & slaughtered
    & drowned &
weighted at the river bottom
the boy outflamed the flame
he was becoming

other boys alongside other boys
he appeared to be so much & so many
he swore to sequoia & redwood, "I will not burn you,"
& it was true he would not raze
though the boy had brightened
the lives of the ones he loved & left
through a hole in his chest
& he walked right through
& upward grew
& knew he could walk

the length of floridatexasmissouriohionewyorkcalifornia & back again
   one day

*soon is now son rise up singing one day soon is now son rise up singing one day soon son
is now son rise up singing one day soon is today son rise up swinging one day soon is now
son rise up swinging one day soon is now son rise is today son rise up swinging*

*& swinging* he could hear singing on the other side though he knew he was gone

# HUSH HARBOR

*Charleston, South Carolina*

1.

"What does it mean to see a black church burn?"
  *bear's breech, bluestar*
and, furthermore, I buried my sister
  *hushed, white roses*
&, furthermore, I buried my lover
    and, anyway, he never said, "forgive"
*June-yanked yarrow*
  *barrenwort creeps*
Mary, don't you weep, oh, Mary

2.

and, furthermore, we buried our mother
  *bugbane, bee balm*
"What does it mean to see a black church burn?"
    up Calhoun Street,
up Ravenel Bridge
    And who among us speaks for us all, not
me, too simple,
    too soon to say
just what I feel when black churches

22

3.

burn, the door closing, burn, & furthermore,
     *black-eyed Susan*
And, furthermore, we buried our father
     *June-snatched yarrow*
*hens & chickens, rosettas* between rock
     the hell that crept through our door of ages
     *Jerusalem*
*Sage, Lavender*
     *Cotton, Coreopsis* corners

4.

And, furthermore, I buried my grandson
     *Bearded Iris*
What does it mean when our black blood turns? Lamb's
     *Ear, Texas Sage*
*False Red Yucca,* swat moths away, sinners
and sin. Must we always invite them in?
     *False Indigo*
*Gayfeather, Thrift*
     Must we always invite them in?

5.

And, furthermore, I buried my anguish
      *Coronation*
*Gold* in my palms after rain, & further-
      more, *Violet*
What does it mean when we memorize Psalms
      Or "stand in the way that sinners take," or
*Umbrella Sedge*
      *Joe-Pye Weed*
Or, sparrow over sycamore

6.

*Forget-me-not*, Father, forget-me-not
      Mother, forget
me not, Saints. For You created my in-
      most being, You
knit me together in my mother's womb
      And, furthermore, I buried my husband
*Bamboo, Goutweed*
      *Evening Primrose*
Mother don't you weep, Mother, don't

7.

moan & *Plantain Lily*, widen your shawl
      *Solomon's Seal*
before you tighten it, Come by here, Lord
        Come by here, Lord
What does it mean when our suffering returns?
          twofold, threefold, fourfold, ten—& if they
turn, let us shout
        let us shout, Saints
What shall we shout when our suffering

8.

returns? If they can burn a cross, they can—
      *Lady's Mantle*
burn a church. If they can burn a church, they
can burn *Coral*
      *Bells*. If they can burn *Coral Bells*, they can—
one bullet, two bullet, ten bullet, more
      hushed white roses
*Baby's Breath, Prick-*
      *ly Pear*. I lack nothing.

9.

Blood on a church pew like *Snow in Summer*
        *Dutch Iris, Dead*
*Nettle, Baby's Breath*
        *Delphinium,*
*Queen Anne's Lace.* I lack
        nothing. I shall not
        I shall not
        shovel winter
        snow. No blood on pews,
nor floors, nor stairs at summer's door.

# SNOWBOUND / A RESISTANCE

*/.*

"This is our land," they said

They were all pasteurized
        like the milk, like the germ
that could not survive

        There was blood on the incline
across the smooth, white expanse

Airy gasp & galvanized tin
        the smoke from the smokehouse
deep snow near the back door

*//.*

Birchbark baskets
        snowsuits & boot prints
evaporated with maple syrup

*///.*

Oh, pride—
        snowbank & Father
snowplow & Mother

27

firelight & plume
        weathered bark & scroll

////.

Drift into the kiln
        then I'll rub your feet with snow

/////.

white snow grey snow red snow smoked snow Ohio snow Michigan snow

///// /.

        She lived constantly on the ragged edge of danger
a drifted-over cornfield
        she sank deep into

///// //.

If she could only picture the outcome
        the end of the trek / the Promise
What her people sometimes called "The Other Side"

///// ///.

Womanhood is a lost paradise
The slightest mistake
could bring disaster

///// ////.

Down weakly in a snow bank
she slid into her own self

# ODYSSEUS LEAVES CIRCE

*after Romare Bearden*

his back to her
       offering, her left
in her staying,

having made
       & soothed
his bed, his head

where the dark
       moods sway
& tether white sails

is that broth
       in the bowl
or poison

she's warmed
       for the one
       who'll leave
having rested

       on his side,
in her bed
       on a pig-
       skinned sheet?

30

# THE SUBJECT OF RETREAT

Your black coat is a door
in the storm. The snow
we don't mention
clings to your boots & powders
& puffs. & poof. Goes.
Dust of the fallen. Right here
at home. The ache
of someone gone missing. Walk it off
like a misspoken word.
Mound of snow. Closed door.
I could open it.

Or maybe just, you know—
brush it off.

Then what? The snow
on the other side. The sound
of what I know & your, *no,* inside it.

# YOU DON'T HAVE TO GO TO MARS FOR LOVE
[request to transmit computer originated audio file to terminal unit]


[begin transmission]

For you to be willing. is enough. It exists to the human eye. not as a sphere. but as a colored star. as part of the endless. outnumbering firmament. as the nightly. whispered message. that we may not reach. what inspires us to grasp.



-



Symbiotic relationships. Marriage. It is neither a decree. nor a warning. A kind of invitation. We eat it hungrily. We are famous for it. We leave our parents' home. eager to get on with our lives. & adulthood. We live in the workaday world. We eat. the workaday foods. Soft. soft. boiled eggs. well-cooked. meats.



- -



The man of the house. drinks his coffee. Informed. direct. occasionally. profane. A black t-shirt. & blue jeans. He will have. mixed. feelings. Lemonade. with. vodka. Certainly. he. will. have. rocket ships. One. of the boys.

32

—‑‑

She was glad. to see him. She. introduced. herself.
Not. a ticker‑tape. parade. There were so many. myths.
she was constantly. processing. A tremendous. amount.
of data. That rhythm. She felt hot. & then. she let go. Almost.
all black. She was. devoted.
to the truth. & the memory. in its orbit.
She was. devoted. to the leap. of faith. Certainly.
he had. rocket ships.


‑ ‑ ‑ ‑ ‑


She was not afraid. of breaking things. & that was key.


‑ ‑ ‑ ‑ ‑ ‑


Galaxies passed. He wanted. a family.
He talked about. going to Mars.

- - - - - -

They talked. more. about. outer space.

- - - - - - -

He was not afraid. of breaking things. & that was key.
He would break. himself. if he had to.

- - - - - - - -

It was almost. a joke at first.

Meet me. in outer space!

Meet me. in Tokyo!

In Madrid! In New York! In Los Angeles!

———————————

She wanted. to meet him.
in outer space. A space where. she didn't need.
protection. He said. "It. would. take. six. months. to. get. to. Mars.
if. you. go. there. slowly."

———————————

The mythical life. The charmed. He wanted.
more. than wonder. He was something.
of a takeover artist.

———————————

a lifestyle.
fueled by vodka.

———————————

They started. their future. A propulsion.
She became. his first wife.
They took. more. trips.
Their. first. long. fights. Their. first. child.
They tapped. into a shared. dream.
A small. good. deed.


They began shopping.          for a rocket.
They toasted. like.     every. two. minutes.


To Mars! To Marriage! To Madonna!


    To Abbey Lincoln! To Erykah Badu!


      To Denzel Washington!
        To Ashford & Simpson!


- - - - - - - - - - - - - -


He said. "I'll be damned.
I think we can. build a rocket."

- - - - - - - - - - - - -

Whatever he pursued. he. usually. got.
But what he got. he. sometimes. lost.
Galaxies. passed.

- - - - - - - - - - - - - -

Rockets. can. explode.
Time. to. rethink. Denzel. Washington.
the persistent link. to Erykah Badu.

The pressures.

- - - - - - - - - - - - - -

Mush-rooms. might. save. the world. Indeed.
a handful. in the backseat.
of a rocket ship. It's no secret.
Erykah Badu. is stunning. Abbey Lincoln.

37

can deeply relate.

a break.

- - - - - - - - - - - - - - - - - -

Monogamy. Madonna says. "I think. people will. like it.
or not. like. it." Denzel Washington.
loves it. "You do. what you. have to do.
so you can. do what. you want. to do."

- - - - - - - - - - - - - - - - - -

Like. build a rocket ship.
Nick Ashford agrees.
"To share. your deepest emotions. & your thoughts."

- - - - - - - - - - - - - - - - - -

White stripes. emerge. amid the green.
in one. petri dish.

- - - - - - - - - - - - - - - - - - - - - -

He reflects. on his life.
& how to change it. For a moment.
his tongue. begins to untie. The dish. swarms.
with insects. An interconnected. power shift.

- - - - - - - - - - - - - - - - - - - - - -

A powerful. & symbiotic. relationship.
But what about. the sharp blade.
of autonomy. The empty lab.
Was that a squeak. in the engine.

- - - - - - - - - - - - - - - - - - - - - -

Time to rethink. Erykah Badu. & Abbey Lincoln.
Time to rethink. Denzel Washington.


⁻ ⁻ ⁻ ⁻ ⁻ ⁻ ⁻ ⁻ ⁻ ⁻ ⁻ ⁻ ⁻ ⁻ ⁻ ⁻ ⁻ ⁻ ⁻ ⁻ ⁻ ⁻ ⁻ ⁻


The key to relationships. Vault.
over fallen trees. Infiltrate.
acres of woodland.      Make love.
in rubber boots. Fuse together.
to make. a mushroom.

Part of the answer. is about. learning from.
& adapting. to each other. Part of the answer.
is about. Abbey Lincoln.
& Madonna. & Erykah. Badu.
& Ashford. & Simpson.
& Denzel. Washington.



⁻ ⁻ ⁻ ⁻ ⁻ ⁻ ⁻ ⁻ ⁻ ⁻ ⁻ ⁻ ⁻ ⁻ ⁻ ⁻ ⁻ ⁻ ⁻ ⁻ ⁻ ⁻ ⁻ ⁻


with hunger & speed.      The rocket ship.      exploded.

40

------------------------------

Any launch. changes. everything.
The ultimate outcome.
is love. or hate. Is success. or failure.
Is life. or death.

------------------------------

You don't have to go. to Mars for love.
For you to be willing. is more than enough.

------------------------------

[end transmission]

# THE DREAM DISTRICT / JANUARY

January, I'm lost inside your industrial gray, my
rig at the ready, my truck trucking, its ginormous

tires flat-ironing the road. Vivica Fox's mantra
on the CB radio, *Black Mambo, Black Mambo.*

More white static & fade. No word from the ladies
out there. They know & don't know. They say &

don't say. Don't say, January. I'm driving past
your peculiar highway sign painted: PASADENA.

January, you know I'm nowhere near. Pennsylvania's no
California. & getting lost exhausts me. January, I pull the air

horn on your fog, pull over at a coffeehouse that looks
like a house I know. But where are the woods, the village

& the goddamn snow? All my guilt & shame on the mount
of books & poems I ought to know. "Now, Honey, read this,"

the Tina Turner lookalike owner says, hands me her copy
of an anti-fracking manifesto derived from ancient tea-

brewing rituals. "& by the way, that's all we serve. No coffee
at this coffeehouse. Our specialty is green," Tina says, "grown local

by the community." All those Ts & Es should put me at ease,
but my bearings are lost. Where am I? Pasadena, Pennsylvania?

"Well, make it black & steep it long," I say,
                                        the day is wearing down on me.

# Q.

One of the four Royal Stars is watching over me. Yeah, I'm blessed
in these times of nervous weather. The leaves chill in a bundle then
scatter like police, off to the next doorstep. They don't step, they
don't faze me. These jeans could hold three men. But it's just one of
me, girl. Only Son. Only Sound. Only Seer. All this green to gold
to red to orange is just theater. I'm the Real. Keep your eyes on the
Navigator of Snow & Infinite Gray. I rock these boots all year. What
a storm got to do with me? Who knows the number of strolls to
heaven? Not that I'm thinking on it. The Heavens know my real name.
But you can call me Q. Quicker than Q. But, anyway. Certain things
a man keeps to himself. Jesus wept. So I don't. The past is for people
who like to play things over & over. Me, I'm on to the next song.
Listen to my own Head Symphony, to the Royal Stars. The colors,
they thrill me, they fuel these legs.

# "I was seduced by the independence of his mind"

*after Bahiana by Maître Parfumeur et Gantier*

You never wear cologne. You give
& you give & you give & you give.
& they take from you. That's their business.
You are mine. Or so you say
with a wink. I want to tell that stupid girl
to shut the hell up about the sonnet.
But you shrug. "Just a girl," you say.
You once saw seabirds in her
skirt, a blue, irregular outline,
a neglected island. & anyway, cologne
is for boys. Just don't
tell their young lovers too soon. Give them
the feathered headdresses & coconuts they imagine,
the little trees that bear chocolate fruit.

# THE SUBJECT OF SURRENDER

I write as the son of a _____. My father was a _____ man,
a _____ man, a _____ - _____ man. He claimed to
love my mother, who _____ & _____ & _____
_____ & _____ until she just disappeared. & who could
blame her? & didn't the rain fall like _____ & didn't the well
of wrongheadedness run deep? My three sisters saw right through
our father's trouble. He was a man who hated to be seen that way.
My father had no choice but to _____. At first, they accepted
his anger. Little did my father know _____, the meaning of
hubris. A man can only _____ for so long. To say nothing of
temperament. There are many _____ on the other side of fear.
& none of them are love. It's time, brothers. A woman sits quietly
thinking. & that's the cold, hard fact of it. Her turning. Her _____,
& her _____, & her _____, the sly mechanics of her
strength gone unacknowledged. My father believed his little yes-men.
His little yes-thoughts. Yeses lead lone men to bleeding. To _____,
& to _____, & to _____. I will pay for what my father
passed on: the _____ & the _____. No, I don't
_____ & expect _____. No, I don't _____. No, I
don't _____ & expect _____. My sisters walked off to
_____. My father thought he could wreck the house & they'd
clean after him. No, I don't _____ & expect anyone to pay
ransom. All those convenient kerchiefs for kidnapped women in
cinema? My father couldn't imagine his hands tied so tightly. My

darling, turn of a woman, I know you will never _____. Let alone read this. I am nothing if not my father's son.

# THE SONNET DISTRICT

"Stay woke," my ex whispered, easing into boxer shorts
& skittering from bed sheets to backdoor, steeplechasing

the furniture in less than sixty seconds. Turns out he'd been working
for the Federal Bureau of Invisible Women & his real name wasn't Tyrone,

which I should have known because when was the last time
I'd met a Tyrone in the black-hole atmosphere of post- & -ish?

Turns out I'd been somnambulating most of my adult life with nary a hint
of productive suspiciousness. Turns out I'd been wooed by the red-wine

rhythms of inebriated verse scrawled on napkins & slipped across
the close-quartered dinner tables of out-of-the-way restaurants.

This I'd confessed to a rapt audience of new polygamists & wayward nuns
at the Center for Alternative Shakespeareans & On-Again-Off-Again

schizophrenics. How could I explain? I was filled with supercelestial longing
& addiction to touch. Just the brush of my ex's arm against mine reduced me

to speechlessness, to say nothing of his dark ties & fine tailored suits falling
to the floor of my bedroom. Things got out of hand when I couldn't

leave him without saying goodbye fourteen times, the stereospecific sparkle
of my manicure holding his chin steady beneath his closed eyes. How could I

have known the FBIW had amended its founding policies & taken to hiring men?
How could I have known the slippery slope of sentimentality would land me

in a leather straitjacket & kitten heels smashing discarded cigarettes
into interrogation room tile? "That string of strangulations in the Chauvinist
    District?"

(My audience leaned in closer then) "I can't call it." But you best believe
there's a spiritualizing pattern coming into alignment, the dazzling intuition

of my female species systematically undermined for the sake of a male leader.
Of course, I stole my files to burn later. The guards were distracted by the
    swing

of their own voices, all "mistress' eyes" & "sun." You best believe
I peeped the conveniently placed escape hatch in the shape of a narrow couplet

from where I sat.
                    It didn't take a telescope to find that.

# POSTING BAIL

"Keep missing me," you say. *Armchair, stepstool, tree stump, church pew,* I'm thinking up a list, half listening. "Sit back & hold still," I tell you. My list is lacking. "Sooner or later," I say, "you'll come up on the Sheriff." & by April, the Bondsman on the fourth floor. *Sofa, swivel, chaise.* He'll be waiting for the right answer, some hint of repentance or pencil-skirted decorum, of a straight-backed, arm-rested, ghost of a former tea-cup tipping self. "You'll have to meet," he'll say with a twist of his belt, "certain conditions." You'll think of your cousin by marriage then. The one who insisted you "meet certain conditions." The one who wanted so badly to act like a man. "Call this number & that number on this day & that. Then maybe I'll help you," your cousin by marriage said. Apparently, men make ultimatums. & operate under certain conditions. & look women in the eye & say, "be more professional," like your cousin in manface. Like the Bondsman. "What's my deadline," you mutter to no one in particular, hoping to change the subject, leaning back in your chair.

# THE DREAM DISTRICT / ORIGINS

*Why did you come here?* A God-awful color.    My grief

*Does God have a face?* I came here to live.    made me

*How much do you care?* Champagne spills nightly.  My groove

*Does champagne spill here?* I care enough.    made me Annie Laura

*How could you doubt me?* Your eyelids look swollen.

*Was I weeping?* I doubted you daily.

*How do you feel?* The dance floor tilted.

*Do dance floors tilt?* The answer frightens me.

*What have you eaten?* Fall & winter moons.    made me eat & eat &
                            eat

*Mars at opposition?* The sky since dusk.

                       tomatoes & cucumbers
                       drizzled with vinegar
                       speckled with pepper

                       made me pork bacon in a
                       cast iron skillet

...

                                        made me pigs' feet

                    ...

                                        made me penny candy

              ...

                                        made me shopkeepers wary

*Were you ashamed?* Dr. King's speeches.

*First Lady Obama's.* "We people
                    who are darker than blue."

                                        made me Chapstick

                                        made me halter tops too
                                        telling

*Why did you come here?* Only god can hold
                    a blasted angel.

*Or banish him or love*  I came here to—
*him again or lift him up.*         —intactness.

                                        made me not telling

*The trace of something left undone?* Nina Simone.

*You also heard her?* I came here to finish.

                                        made me John 3:16
                                        made me baptism
*You recognized my hair?* A chronic hangover.

*You drank the wine?* Soft kinks & sure shine.

                                            made me bad
                                            perms

*Why did you come here?* Mount Everest, Kanchenjunga.

*You've climbed the overlook?* I came here to die.

                                            made me the car
                                            my mother couldn't afford
                                            made me late payments

*Were you left alone?* The postage stamps yellowed.   made me a key
                                            hung round my neck

*You wanted to write letters?* When no one was home
                              I stole inks & papers.

*Were you ashamed?*    Malcolm X.                     made me "you black"

*Tina Turner's interview?* "I don't ever remember
                              being called a nigger..."

*Why did you come here?* Pollen from an Easter lily.   made me "you look like
                                            your Aunt Theresa"

*How many filled the chapel?* I came here to grieve.

*How have you changed?* He cracked a speckled egg.   made me cut grass &
                                            allergies

*Quail eggs keep here?* I no longer worry.

*Could you love another?* Lemon trees flourish.      made me my father's strikes
                                                     at the chemical plant
*Will the trees bare lemons?* Love made me weary.


*Your parents sacrificed?* Someone left the gate open.  made me picket lines

*Will you close the gate?* Like their parents before them.


*What do you regret?* Look south before dawn.     made me No *scabs!*

*& tomorrow north?* "I'm not ready to be bereaved."


*Were you ashamed?* Edna Lewis.                  made me a Duncan Hines
                                              cake
*How gently did you lift your eyebrows?*
                              "& the few times I was,
                              it didn't bother me."

*Why did you come here?* Crystalized sugar      made me ten weeping
                        on jar-hung string.     candles

*The string tied to a pencil?* I came here to live.


*Why did you come here?* Three dark scratches.     made me a prayer
                                        an unplanned  presence
*Was the creature declawed?* I came here to live.

*Why did you come here?* "Worry gives small things     made me fingers
                      big shadows."                    crossed &
                                                       maybes

*The ferocity of your hands.* I came here to live.


*Why did you come here?* "The chart wants to reveal itself made me sugar
                           as a living thing."     made me salt
*You've met the seer?* I came here to live.


*Why did you come here?* "this goes out               not enough
                      to all the baby mamas..."       frosting


*You miss her deeply?* How can it be that she's gone
                           & I live?                  made me a paper
                                                      plate licked clean

# THE FROG DISTRICT

I zipped my wetsuit & flopped
from the edge of a queen-sized bed,
into the deep; which is to say I turned
in my sleep & swam to the pond
where no one recognized me, away
from the faithless & careless, toward
the skulls of monks who ground
their jawbones & moaned:
*We're born & we die. We once swam*
*where you swim.* Excuse me? Had I
needed reminding? More
amphibian than queen, more mad
than merry, the after-anger of frog work
treaded inside me. I had netted fish, I had
scrubbed algae, I had shaken the speckled remains
of food from lava-colored castles.

*All you had to do was ask,* whispered
unlifted fingers. Bubble talk.
But let me not trouble those waters.
My story leaps elsewhere, spider-webbed
emerald-eyed, post-weary. I kick
my way back top. Bye-bye, Froggy
Bottom. Keep your convenient book
of procedural treasures, your lectures

above the wellsprings, your bit of
eerie swampland & half-breed
mermaids wrecking toy ships.

# CUTTHROAT / THE RISING COST OF FUEL

Dead tired     no need
to dream—
      —ring—


    you—
—dead—
     —sister—


telephone—
in—
your—
—palm—my—
—our—nails
gnawed nubs
thinking—
—of—
calling—
—calling
but not—

          —she's— you're—
          beside—
          me—

             us—

                              right—
                              here—
                              —you—
                              —her


busy     tired
worn—
—out—
out—out—re—
—heating—regarding—
take—out—reheating
—out—it's take out—in—


an undecorated kitchen


                              alone—
                        —where
                          you—I—
                        we—
                        —left—me—
                        her—
                              waiting—
                              ring—
                ring—but—don't—
                              sleep—

59

she—we—
I—never—
answered—

at least    you—I
told—
tell myself—wrecked
        twitching
in your—my—
our—own—
empty head
        wrecked—

the ghouls of dinner—
plates—pots—
ghosted—greased—
the grime—of
being used

so—wipe—
it  her   them
away—

twitch & turn—your

digital head                    separate needs

a few feet—miles—
from us—me—we—you—
which—

—galaxies—

when it gets this busy, this bleak
too viscid to touch directly,

gloves—
heels—
stir—
r—rups—
gel—pinch—
—sit—
—hymns—pills
chills
it's time—

the  oncoming
hollowed out howl
dead sister—
—howl—

receiver—you—
but—I—
        you—
we—
        had to—
go—you
—you—I—
we—
hung  up

you—I—

couldn't sleep & woke every hour & tried to explain
the almost dead to the living, but too late—

a call—something about prescription meds & bombs
in the Middle East  & credit card fees & gas prices what

they—you—
we—are—
—were—we—
—are enough

Anything would will set me you us off

You—I
—could—
shove—I  could—
—stab I could
grab—

there are black women in laundromats
& psych wards drowning babies tethered

weak with the numbers rolling over
like another one of us in the grave

with the beetles & the mourning
approaching in a gold limousine

you—
we—
I—

climbed  in & sat across from our your my mother
wide awake & excused from answering everyone for a while.

# DARK AND LOVELY AFTER TAKEOFF (A FUTURE)

Nobody straightens their hair anymore.
Space trips & limited air supplies will get you conscious quick.

My shea-buttered braids glow planetary
as I turn unconcerned, unburned by the pre-take-off bother.

"Leave it all behind," my mother'd told me,
sweeping the last specs of copper thread from her front porch steps &

just as quick, she turned her back to me. Why
had she disappeared so suddenly behind that earthly door?

"Our people have made progress, but, perhaps,"
she'd said once, "not enough to guarantee safe voyage

to the Great Beyond," beyond where Jesus
walked, rose, & ascended in the biblical tales that survived

above sprocket-punctured skylines &
desert-dusted runways jeweled with wrenches & sheet metal scraps.

She'd no doubt exhale with relief to know
ancient practice & belief died hard among the privileged, too.

Hundreds of missions passed & failed, but here
I was strapped in my seat, anticipating—what exactly?

Curved in prayer or remembrance of a hurt
so deep I couldn't speak. Had that been me slammed to the ground, cuffed,

bulleted with pain as I danced with pain
I couldn't shake loose, even as the cops aimed pistols at me,

my body & mind both disconnected
& connected & unable to freeze, though they shouted "Freeze!"

like actors did on bad television.
They'd watched & thought they recognized me, generic or bland,

without my mother weeping like Mary,
Ruby, Idella, Geneava, or Ester stunned with a grief

our own countrymen refused to see, to
acknowledge or cease initiating, instigating, &

even mocking in the social networks,
ignorant frays bent & twisted like our DNA denied

but thriving & evident nonetheless—
You better believe the last things I saw when far off lifted

were *Africa Africa Africa*
*Africa Africa Africa Africa Africa* . . .

& though it pained me to say it sooner:
the unmistakable absence of the Great Barrier Reef.

# THEREISNOCENTEROFTHEUNIVERSE

"Because they were dirty and Black and obnoxious and Black and arrogant and Black and poor and Black and Black and Black and Black."
—Audre Lorde

thereisnocenteroftheuniversethereisnocenteroftheuniverse
thereisnocenteroftheuniversethereisnocenteroftheuniverse
thereisnocenteroftheuniversethereisnocenteroftheuniverse
thereisnocenteroftheuniversethereisnocenteroftheuniverse
thereisnocenteroftheuniversethereisnocenteroftheuniverse
thereisnocenteroftheuniversethereisnocenteroftheuniverse
thereisnocenteroftheuniversethereisnocenteroftheuniverse
thereisnocenteroftheuniversethereisnocenteroftheuniverse
thereisnocenteroftheuniversethereisnocenteroftheuniverse
thereisnocenteroftheuniversethereisnocenteroftheuniverse
thereisnocenteroftheuniversethereisnocenteroftheuniverse
thereisnocenteroftheuniversethereisnocenteroftheuniverse
thereisnocenteroftheuniversethereisnocenteroftheuniverse
thereisnocenteroftheuniversethereisnocenteroftheuniverse
thereisnocenteroftheuniversethereisnocenteroftheuniverse
thereisnocenteroftheuniversethereisnocenteroftheuniverse
thereisnocenteroftheuniversethereisnocenteroftheuniverse
thereisnocenteroftheuniversethereisnocenteroftheuniverse
thereisnocenteroftheuniversethereisnocenteroftheuniverse
thereisnocenteroftheuniversethereisnocenteroftheuniverse
thereisnocenteroftheuniversethereisnocenteroftheuniverse
thereisnocenteroftheuniversethereisnocenteroftheuniverse
thereisnocenteroftheuniversethereisnocenteroftheuniverse
thereisnocenteroftheuniversethereisnocenteroftheuniverse
thereisnocenteroftheuniversethereisnocenteroftheuniverse
thereisnocenteroftheuniversethereisnocenteroftheuniverse

# THE RIVER WANDERER

There was a river turned to   Goddess.     Was kin to river turned to Flame.

    As a child I dreamt that river. None could   keep me from that vision.

They lowered me in the Mighty Waters. Lowered me in the Creek of Shame.

    Others tried the Brook of Whispers. None could save me. None

    could save me.

Still I dreamt the River Snowdrift. To my kin I made no sense. *Those folks*

    *out   there shall never love you,* said my Preacher. Said my Pa. Still

I shivered when I     wakened. *(Ganga of Glaciers, Ganga of Snow).* Left with

    Mama's

    only bread. Left to find the cold that called me:     *You my sister.*

*You, my sister. Come now sister, ashes & all. (Ganga of Glaciers, Ganga of Snow, Ganga*

    *of Forgiven).*

    Wash me now, sister. Rest my shoulder on the shore. Lift my ashes

to your   sky. Once our Mama raised our arms: so we could speak the

    sacred tongues.

    To speak in tongues was to     relent. To call the water that

    would drown us—

firmament. Torrent, let go.     Torrent, let go. I'll meet you at the River's

    Bottom,

dressed in silver scales with fin. You'll clutch      my hand,

we'll swim in circles.

Taunt the serpents, taunt the sharks. & when the glaciers get to   melting,

all God's Rivers we shall haunt. All God's Rivers we shall haunt.

ACKNOWLEDGMENTS

Deepest gratitude to these publications and institutions:
*The Book of Scented Things*, the Carnegie Museum of Art, *Crashtest Magazine*, *Fledgling Rag*, *Huizache*, *Letters to the Future: Black Women / Radical Writing*, *Los Angeles Review*, *Poem-A-Day*, *Poetry*, *The Spectacle*, *Spiral Orb*, *THIS*, and *The Volta Book of Poets*.

"Snowbound / A Resistance" is a found poem and response to the young adult novel *Snowbound in Hidden Valley* by Holly Wilson.

"Q." was inspired by a prompt from fiction writer Sherrie Flick, who plays hard and works hard and through her friendship taught me the difference.

A special thank you to Ingrid Schaffner and Liz Park, curator and associate curator of the Carnegie International, 57th Edition, whose brilliant execution of the Tam O'Shanter Drawing Sessions breathed life back into this book.

Thanks for your wisdom when I lost my way: Burns Fam; Harvey Fam (Crystal and Tasha); Toi Derricotte; Erika Asikoye; Francis "Serg" Rachal; Sandyha Rajan; Dr. Tuajuanda C. Jordan, Dr. Michael S. Glaser, and the St. Mary's College of Maryland Lucille Clifton Award organizers; Douglas Kearney; Shara McCallum; Marta Lucia Vargas; Afaa Michael Weaver; and Crystal Williams. Thank you, Terrance Hayes.

Thank you, Martha Rhodes, Ryan Murphy, Sally Ball, and the Four Way Books team.

Yona Harvey is an American poet and recipient of the the Kate Tufts Discovery Award for her first poetry collection, *Hemming the Water*. She is among the first black women to write for Marvel Comics since the company's founding in 1939 and the first black woman to write for the Marvel character Storm. She facilitates creative writing workshops, delivers writing-specific speaker topics, and has worked with teenagers writing about mental health issues in collaboration with *Creative Nonfiction* magazine. Her website is yonaharvey.com.

Publication of this book was made possible by grants and donations. We are also grateful to those individuals who participated in our 2019 Build a Book Program. They are:

Anonymous (14), Sally Ball, Vincent Bell, Jan Bender-Zanoni, Laurel Blossom, Adam Bohannon, Lee Briccetti, Jane Martha Brox, Anthony Cappo, Carla & Steven Carlson, Andrea Cohen, Janet S. Crossen, Marjorie Deninger, Patrick Donnelly, Charles Douthat, Morgan Driscoll, Lynn Emanuel, Blas Falconer, Monica Ferrell, Joan Fishbein, Jennifer Franklin, Sarah Freligh, Helen Fremont & Donna Thagard, Ryan George, Panio Gianopoulos, Lauri Grossman, Julia Guez, Naomi Guttman & Jonathan Mead, Steven Haas, Bill & Cam Hardy, Lori Hauser, Bill Holgate, Deming Holleran, Piotr Holysz, Nathaniel Hutner, Elizabeth Jackson, Rebecca Kaiser Gibson, Dorothy Tapper Goldman, Voki Kalfayan, David Lee, Howard Levy, Owen Lewis, Jennifer Litt, Sara London & Dean Albarelli, David Long, Ralph & Mary Ann Lowen, Jacquelyn Malone, Fred Marchant, Donna Masini, Louise Mathias, Catherine McArthur, Nathan McClain, Richard McCormick, Kamilah Aisha Moon, James Moore, Beth Morris, John Murillo & Nicole Sealey, Kimberly Nunes, Rebecca Okrent, Jill Pearlman, Marcia & Chris Pelletiere, Maya Pindyck, Megan Pinto, Barbara Preminger, Kevin Prufer, Martha Rhodes, Paula Rhodes, Silvia Rosales, Linda Safyan, Peter & Jill Schireson, Jason Schneiderman, Roni & Richard Schotter, Jane Scovell, Andrew Seligsohn & Martina Anderson, Soraya Shalforoosh, Julie A. Sheehan, James Snyder & Krista Fragos, Alice St. Claire-Long, Megan Staffel, Marjorie & Lew Tesser, Boris Thomas, Pauline Uchmanowicz, Connie Voisine, Martha Webster & Robert Fuentes, Calvin Wei, Bill Wenthe, Allison Benis White, Michelle Whittaker, Rachel Wolff, and Anton Yakovlev.